Puffer has Pinkeye!!!

Written and Photographed by:

Diane Baxter Trapeni

Keep an eye out for these other exciting titles:

Nellie the Nibbler

Alice the Guinea Pig

Penny the Python

Jeremiah, a Song Bird

Vincent (Christmas reindeer)

Hubert

Phil Harmonic

Jeff Sticks up for his Buddies

Cord, Glue and 8 Screws

Sydney Has Friends

DEDICATION

To Amber and her wonderful family.

The children are learning to be clean

and safe just like Puffer is.

DMBT

Puffer woke up groggy and couldn't open his eyes! His eyes were stuck together with sticky eye stuff…YUCK!

He wiped his eyes on some seaweed and looked in the mirror. PINKEYE!!! He looked like a ghoulish monster!!!

He swam down to his treasure chest to get his eye drops. He couldn't go to school with Pinkeye!!! He'd have to stay home a whole day!!!

He must have searched for 15 minutes or an hour for those drops. They were a special medicine for Pinkeye. He even dumped the chest over!!!

He finally found the drops and put
one drop in each eye to start.
Aw…he felt better almost
immediately…He wondered how he
even got the Pinkeye at all…

Did he get too close to Betty? She had it last week. Did he forget to wash his flippers after using the bathroom?
Did he touch a dirty knob or faucet? He wasn't sure how he got it but he knew one thing for sure...He'd wash up better...and often...just like teacher said!!!

Puffer had to stay home from school for sure. He didn't want to contaminate the others.
So he may as well clean his room.
It was a mess now that he dumped his treasure chest!

He'd scrub the bathroom to make sure Tommy, mommy and daddy wouldn't get Pinkeye too!

Puffer would have to stay away from his baby brother, Tommy, today. That made him the saddest. He loved playing with his baby brother. He was showing him how to "blow up" into a prickly balloon for protection!

So Puffer would have to remember…
to wash his flippers often…

He couldn't share glasses or cups with
anyone and never rub his eyes…

After all, you can't be TOO CAREFUL!!!

Story 2:
Puffer stopped playing mean tricks on Shrimp.
They became friends after that cleaning incident.

In fact, to keep busy, Puffer got a pen pal in Texas!

His name is Henry.

Henry is a horned lizard.

Henry's body is covered with sharp prickles just like Puffer's is… especially when he is afraid of getting EATEN!

Puffer can enlarge like a balloon by sucking in water.
He gets so big and thorny, no one can or wants to eat him.
(Hahahahahah, funny story.)

The pals have a lot in common really. They have even more differences though. Henry lives on land. Puffer is a sea creature. Puffer has fins and Henry has 4 legs. However, they both have a rather prickly attitude sometimes. (Don't we all.)

Someday, they hope to meet or at least see each other on their computers. (They like to make sure you know how modern and up-to-date they are!).

It's nice to have such a friend as Henry. Knowing him has expanded Puffer's universe. He has never been on land in the scorching sun but he can visualize it after reading Henry's letters

Henry feels the same about Puffer's water adventure journeys. He feels cooler just imagining the ocean and all the diverse creatures inside. They know they'll be friends forever. They want to learn all they can about the "other" worlds.

I bet you want to explore other places and diverse peoples too. Let's do it!!!

We'll meet back here and exchange stories and pictures of our newest adventures.

See you in one year. Same day…same time. I'll wait for you.

The End

(Life is teeming with unlikely

possibilities!)

Keep an eye out for these other exciting Children's Books:

Dot and Comma with Friends

Floyd the Colorful Chameleon

Francesca the Tropical Red-eyed Green Frog

Joe's Got Spots

Merrill the Squirrel and Jen the Hen:

Part 6 Brittany's Back!!!

Christmas at the Mountain Top Inn and Resort

A Three Piggie Circus

Frances, a Gifted Frog for Sure!

Saffire. (Butterfly)

Serendipity. (Fish)

Big Louie's Dead (But not Forgotten)

Christmas at the Castle

We are proud to introduce:

Raven Learns a Hard Lesson

Raven has a family problem. She steals everything that takes her fancy…anything shiny and pretty. See what happened at school. Enjoy!

About the TrapStone LLC: Owner and Author…

My name is Miss Diane. I taught for 42 years and have read thousands of books aloud to children.

I enjoyed that so much, I decided to write and illustrate books for you myself.

Enjoy!!!

Ken Stone Sr. is a computer programmer and a business partner extraordinaire. He put my words, pictures and computer magic together so you could meet… Puffer has Pinkeye and Puffer Gets a Penpal.

www.ingramcontent.com/pod-product-compliance
Lightning Source LLC
Chambersburg PA
CBHW042127110726
48006CB00003B/799